Have a Good Week

FAYE MUNNINGS

Copyright © 2025 by Faye Munnings

All rights reserved. No part of this publication may be reproduced, stored in a retrieval system, or transmitted in any form or by any means—electronic, mechanical, photocopying, recording, or otherwise—without prior written permission from the author, except for brief excerpts used in reviews or educational purposes under fair use guidelines.

First Printing: 2025

Dedication

Dedicated to *Helen Munnings* and *Dwayne Munnings*.

Table of Contents

The Manufacturer Knows 1

Infrastructure Week 2

Mirror, Mirror, What Can I Be? 3

Who Told You That You Were Naked? 4

Pray For The Underbelly 5

That Don't Make No Sense 6

Shot-Gun 7

Strech-Out 8

El Roi, the God Who Sees Me 9

They Are Already Comfortable, Let Them Pray 10

Are We To Live In Poverty? 11

Like the Father, So Are the Children 12

A Righteous Courtship 13

The Power And The Right 14

Name Drop 15

Can We Touch Our Toes? 16

Even If It's Many and Very 17

The Three R's 19

If It Doesn't Look Like The Promise... 21

And Then Digest 22

This Simple Message 23

Now, That's The Key 24
Grace Upon Grace, Favor Upon Favor 25
Let This Be Your Help 26
There Is A Scripture For That 27
Drop Down and Give Me Fifty 28
Majority Rules 29
Poetry Man 30
Our Greatest Tool 31

The Manufacturer Knows

One day, I found myself outside in the rain and lightning. My hands were full, so I could not carry everything to my car and unlock the door. As I approached my car, I realized that I didn't have my key handy. It was buried deep in my pocket. I began to feel anxious. I forgot that my car would open if I touched the handle because it sensed the key. For us, let the challenges in our lives know what is deep in our spiritual pockets. We don't have to get anxious or overwhelmed. Just as my key was deep in my pocket and its power was activated, God's word is available to us. You see, it wasn't difficult for me to get inside my car. The car manufacturer already made a way for moments like that. The same goes for us, God is our manufacturer and knew we would be challenged and has made a way of escape. We don't have to struggle for the key.

1 Corinthians 10:13 tells us He will provide a way of escape.

Have a good week. ☺

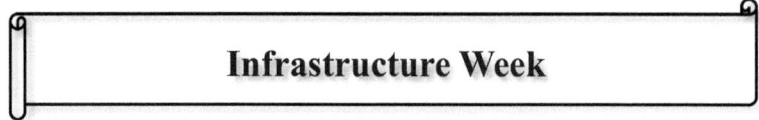

Infrastructure Week

There is a local organization that relies solely on donations for its operations. Their system for collecting small sums is easy and straightforward, but they lack a mechanism for receiving larger donations. Moreover, when anyone calls asking for information on making large dollar donations, calls are not returned. (no words). It appears the organization does not anticipate receiving large donations; if they did, there would be a system in place for it. This has prompted me to inquire about our ability to receive on a larger scale and let this be a lesson for us. Let's not underestimate what can show up in our lives. Let's not pray small and believe small. Make room.

1 Corinthians 2:9 says,

> *"Eye has not seen, nor ear heard, Nor have entered into the heart of man The things which God has prepared for those who love Him."*

Have our hearts and our internal infrastructure ready to receive and …

Have a good week. ☺

Mirror, Mirror, What Can I Be?

God leaves little hints all around us, and a flowing river is a perfect example of His design for our lives. Just as blood flows through our veins to keep us alive, a river keeps flowing to stay vibrant and healthy. When the river's flow stops, the river dies. Just as if our blood stops, it clots and puts our lives at risk.

If we value money, influence, or anything else, we need to let it flow. These things aren't intended to be hoarded or held tightly in fear. They are meant to be shared. When we hold the grip so tightly, we smother the very thing we crave. Therefore, be like a river, keep moving, keep flowing. Remember, when you look into a river, you see your own reflection. Let that reflection remind you to mirror that which you aspire to be.

"so, where the river flows, everything will live."

~ Ezekiel 47:9.

Have a good week. ☺

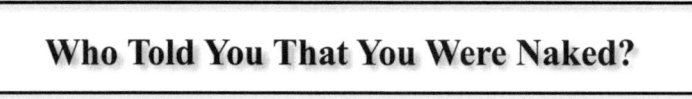

Who Told You That You Were Naked?

It's important for us to reflect on what narratives and influences are shaping our perception of ourselves. What messages have we internalized or unknowingly absorbed that led to feelings of shame, guilt, inadequacy, or it's too lateness? God provides help. We see in

> "Blessed is the one who finds wisdom, and the one who gets understanding."
>
> ~ Proverbs 3:13

Let's remember, if something is making us feel weak, exposed, or not as beautiful as a flower in bloom, then we need to ask, who told me that I was naked? Or sees me less than who God made me to be? Our response should be that I'm not defined by others' identity of me. I have been created with purpose and worth. I am seen and I am cared for.

In other words, I have been redeemed. I've been given a beautiful coat of many colors, just like Joseph, and it's wrapped all around me.

Have a good week. 😊

Pray For The Underbelly

Circumstances may, at times, overpower our faith. As depicted in Mark chapter 9, we encounter a father who exclaims with conviction, 'I believe, but help me with my unbelief.' Many of us have experienced such moments. This week, pray beneath the promises, what I call the underbelly. Our faith is the foundation.

However, sometimes, we don't have enough faith. You see, if we apply the promises onto a weak foundation, then the promised results can't stand. Therefore, plunge into the bedrock of our anxieties, uncertainties, and feelings of unworthiness. Engage in prayer with the Father, acknowledging, 'I believe,' and yet, I yearn to believe even more. Simply say, please, Father, help me with my unbelief.' Then, await an opportunity to experience the Lord's delightful presence and walk forward within His promises.

Have a good week. ☺

That Don't Make No Sense

In order to experience a breakthrough, we should allow our hearts to guide the tenor of our prayers. This process may require us to suspend our reliance on logical reasoning.

As Proverbs 3: 5 aptly advises,

> *"Trust in the Lord with all your heart and lean not to your own understanding."*

In essence, prioritize the promptings of our heart in prayer and step aside. God is not constrained by the limitations of human logic; instead, He is moved by the sincerity of our heartfelt prayers. Therefore, let us resolve to engage in prayer from the depths of our hearts, tempering our reliance on logic with an unyielding faith. As members of the Radical Faith Gang, we are united by our commitment to embracing an unwavering trust in God, even if our answered prayers don't make a bit of sense!

Have a good week. 😊

Shot-Gun

It is widely acknowledged that we should pray without ceasing. As prayer is a reciprocal interaction, this suggests that God also prays without ceasing. This concept is thought-provoking. In essence, God is engaged in perpetual prayer alongside us. Additionally, He longs for us. It is His heartfelt desire to spend time with us. Envision the creator of the universe yearning for us. He could have anything, yet it is us for whom He desires to pray. He wants to reconcile us back to Himself.

Hence, if we ever have negative thoughts about ourselves, we should remember that the same hand who created the sun and the moon, also created us. That same righteous right hand is destined to uphold us in times of need, as promised in Isaiah 41. Therefore, go ahead and pray without ceasing. Because He is at the ready, riding shot-gun right beside us.

Have a good week. 😊

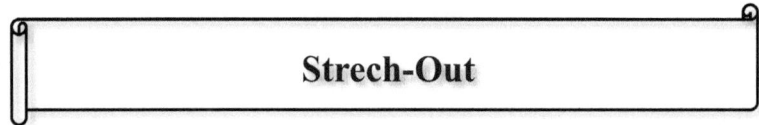

Strech-Out

Does our faith ever face circumstances that test our belief to the point of almost breaking? Throughout our lives, we may be called upon to expand our faith, which may involve enduring challenging life situations that require our submission and even venturing into uncharted territory. We recognize that God is present when our faith needs to be stretched and strengthened. He knows that we are incapable of facing this stretch without His assistance. As a reference, we read in Matthew 12 about a man with a withered hand; he was asked to stretch out his hand for it to be restored.

The stretching out of his hand was when it was restored. So, we must also stretch out our faith to be renewed. Let us take a moment for prayer. Dear God, we are aware that our faith may be tested. There is no tribulation that You are incapable of guiding us through. We pledge to eliminate any obstacles that we may have erected, such as doubt, fear, and worry. Therefore, we draw inspiration from 2 Timothy 1:7, which states,

"For God hath not given us the spirit of fear; but of power, and of love, and of a sound mind."

Consequently, we anticipate Your help and deliverance as we stretch towards our newness. Amen.

El Roi, the God Who Sees Me

One can find oneself amidst a multitude yet experience profound invisibility, possibly facing rejection and a sudden desire to leave. This parallels the relationship between Sarah and Hagar in the Bible. Sarah requested Hagar's assistance, yet Hagar was the one ostracized and banished to the desert. Has anyone ever experienced a similar situation? One tries to be helpful, yet the one seeking help becomes offended.

Nevertheless, we can glean wisdom from Sarah and Hagar's story. Though Sarah becomes displeased with Hagar and expels her to the wilderness, it is within this displacement that God delivers the ultimate assurance to Hagar. There, God declares, *'I have heard the boy's cry, and from him a great nation shall arise; he shall be the ancestor of kings.'* Let this be helpful to us. In the place of rejection, failed marriages, infertility, health issues, financial despair, lost dreams, etc.

God still has a promise for us. This week, call on *"El Roi, the God who sees me."* No matter our current placement, we know He has given us a promise. A promise to prosper us and not harm us. A plan for hope and a future. With that, stand on the word of God. Even if you can't find Him, He can find you. (see Jeremiah 29:11).

Have a good week. ☺

They Are Already Comfortable, Let Them Pray

Hello, my friend! I heard about a husband who was despondent because his wife was near death. The doctors said there was nothing more they could do. The husband listened to the doctors and accepted what he was told. Ultimately, he called his church members, and one brother felt stirred to pray for a full recovery. The believing brother asked his prayer partners to join him in prayer. However, the partner's prayers were based on her dying. However, the one faithful brother continued to pray that his friend's wife would live. As you would know, the wife fully recovered and even outlived her husband for many years. For us this week, continue to pray as you are prompted. No matter the circumstance.

James 5:14 says,

> "Is anyone among you sick? Let him call for the church elders, and let them pray over him."

If your faith fails you, call on friends who have radical faith. You know, the ones who, on other occasions, make you shake your head and wonder what they are doing now. Usually, they are already comfortable defying logic. You should let them pray.

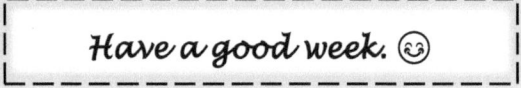

Are We To Live In Poverty?

What is the theological viewpoint on poverty? I firmly believe that God does not intend for us to be perpetually impoverished. While some may find themselves in such a situation, God does not desire for us to remain in that state. Whether it's financial, health, social, relational, or any other type of poverty, God wants to move us out.

As Isaiah 41:17 says,

> *"The poor and needy search for water, but there is none. Yet, I, the LORD, will answer them; I, the God of Israel, will not forsake them."*

Our Father is fully aware of our situations and is committed to making a way for us to escape.

He will extend His righteous right hand to all who diligently seek Him. Therefore, if anyone tries to convince us that we are destined to endure perpetual poverty, kindly remind them who our Father is!

Have a good week. 😊

Like the Father, So Are the Children

If you have ever felt desolate, empty, and despairing, take comfort in knowing that God has also experienced these very same conditions. As recorded in Genesis, in the beginning, the earth was formless, dark, and void. However, God responded by initiating a series of pronouncements beginning with the phrase *"Let there be."* He then declared it good. Let us follow suit and speak a prophetic word over our lives. If the earth can appear to be formless, dark, and empty, so can we. The truth is, during the initial dark times of the earth, the spirit of God was hovering; we need to have peace knowing that God is hovering over us, too. If we find ourselves in this situation, we can respond just like the Father did. Proclaim what it shall be!

Have a good week. ☺

A Righteous Courtship

God's eternal love is as pure as a breeze on a parched summer day. His love restores our spirit. Let us draw upon this divine affection to allow us to conquer our challenges. Pray this prayer: "Oh, Father, I have exhausted all my known resources, yet I fail to live a life that resonates with my true self. My reality does not mirror how I feel. God, please establish me in my rightful place, as you promised in Ezekiel 37:13. I want to dwell in a space that my soul recognizes and is satisfied. From there, I shall rejoice, knowing that you have spoken and fulfilled your promise. I ask that You do this simply because You love me.

'Amen.'

Have a good week. 😊

The Power And The Right

Psalm 20 is a prayer offered on behalf of King David as he prepares for battle. The people asked the Lord to heed David's calls for help, to provide aid, and to offer unwavering support from Zion. They requested that the Lord grant David's heart's desires and ensure the success of the battle. What the people understood was the power of prayer. Furthermore, they understood the right to offer such a comprehensive prayer with an expectation of success. Let this serve as a reminder to us this week. Offer complete prayers from a position of entitlement. We are children of God, and we have the right to have success.

Have a good week. ☺

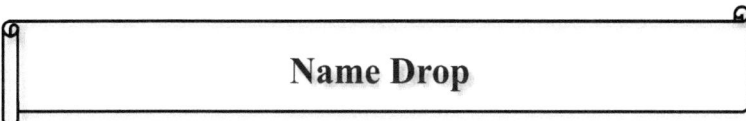

Name Drop

These names of God carry deep meanings and can be powerful to use in specific types of prayers:

El Shaddai ("God Almighty"): Call upon this name when you need God's strength and power in a situation.

El Elyon ("Most High God"): Use this name to exalt and praise God, acknowledging His supremacy.

El Gibbor (Gibhor) ("Mighty God"): Pray this name when facing battles or when you seek God's protection and defense for yourself or others.

El Chaiyim ("Living God"): Invoke this name during times involving birth, life, or death, seeking God's life-giving presence.

Jehova Jireh ("The Lord Will Provide"): Pray this name when you are in need or praying for God's provision and redemption for His people.

Jehovah Nissi ("The Lord is My Banner"): Use this name in situations where you need God to lead you to victory, especially when you feel like you're coming from behind or in need of a breakthrough.

These names allow us to connect with God in a focused and purposeful way, aligning prayer with His many attributes.

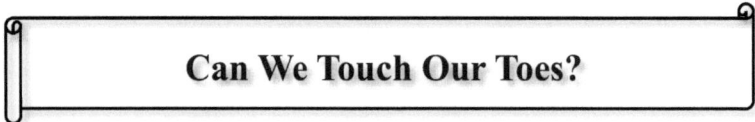

Can We Touch Our Toes?

The antithesis of emptiness is fullness. The aspirational pursuit of the state of feeling full often involves traveling a road less traveled.

How do we get there? Scripture says in Matthew 7:14,

"But small is the gate and narrow the road that leads to life, and only a few find it.".

This tells us that the path is slight and can get missed if we look for the broad, heavily traveled pathway. If an exceptional life is our goal, let us lean into that sliver of space where our faith leads. Be flexible enough to lean on it and rock with it. Don't focus only on our understanding. Stretch and even touch our toes if that's what it takes. Nevertheless, in all our ways, acknowledge God, and He will make our path straight.

Have a good week. ☺

Even If It's Many and Very

Is anyone going through a difficult situation? If so, let's take a lesson from Ezekiel 37. The story goes like this: the Lord's spirit was upon Ezekiel. He set Ezekiel in the middle of a valley of dead, dry bones.

"The Lord walked Ezekiel back and forth, and he saw many bones, and they were very dry. Then the Lord asked Ezekiel, "Can these piles of dry bones live?" And Ezekiel answered, "Lord, only you can answer that question."

Next, God said to Ezekiel, go ahead and prophesy over these dry bones. Tell the dry bones; this is what the Sovereign Lord says. "I will make breath come into you and you will come to life." For us, let us pay attention to what actually happened here. The Lord didn't tell Ezekiel to listen to Him prophesy; He called Ezekiel to speak over the dry bones himself. As we read the chapter, the bones came to life by standing on their feet as vast as an army. These words should excite us. They remind us that our situations may be dead-looking, but we have the authority to speak the words of the sovereign Lord over them. Sometimes, we think, well, only God knows the answer. I agree. He always does. But we are in a relationship with Him. So, don't despair even if it's many and very dry.

Exercise your authority and tell your situation you shall live. Notice that not only did the bones come to life, but they were also strong and vast, like an army. So, our situations can come to life and function like we were privileged.

Now go on and;

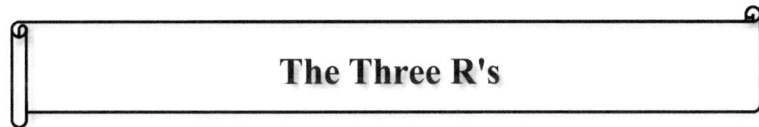

The Three R's

There are many references in scripture that tell us to write down what the Lord shows us. He tells us to write it down because it's so easy to forget. Our busy lives are most likely the culprit.

God speaks to us using many forms, including His word. He provides dreams and visions. Even if you think it is insignificant, write it down. Sometimes, our situations contradict what we think His Word promises. We should understand that we may be at the beginning. Not recognizing that may cause us to lose out on our desired outcome. Writing things down helps us to see the various stages. We can later read what we wrote and clearly see the hand of God at work. We can see His righteousness through our lens of faith. Often, after our circumstances are resolved, we forget the full journey. Writing it down and going back can be a helpful tool.

Additionally, this review can also inspire us to take action!! Often, in scripture, the Lord speaks and then instructs His people to write it down.

Habakkuk 2:2 says,

"Then the Lord answered me and said: "Write the vision

And make it plain on tablets,

That he may run who reads it".

For us, Read, Write and Run-on.

Have a good week. 😊

If It Doesn't Look Like The Promise...

In Deuteronomy 30, we read about prosperity (again) after turning towards the Lord. As we can see, there is a common theme within the scriptures. As we turn toward the Lord, He turns towards us. Week after week, we are reminded of His promises. Therefore, hold on to them. Let them populate in your mind regardless of what is going on within your outside world.

The LORD your God will delight in you and will make you prosperous in all the work of your hands. He simply asks that you turn to Him with all your heart and soul.

Doing this is not too difficult or beyond our reach.

No, the Word is very near us. Deuteronomy 30:17 says,

"..it is in your mouth and in your heart so you may obey it."

Now, for us this week, if it doesn't look like what He promises, then He is not finished with you yet.

Let that encourage you and go forward.

Have a good week. ☺

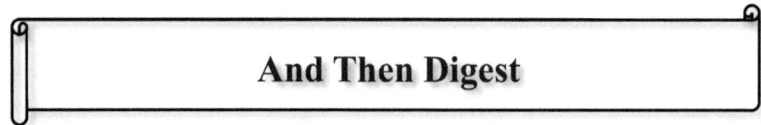

And Then Digest

As we live, we may find ourselves in spaces requiring a different faith level. A faith that calls for a more pronounced speech. A definitive speech. That is because we earned the right to encounter more difficult situations. That may cause you to raise an eyebrow, but if we compare it to some of our other growth experiences, we can see that it makes sense. For example, when we graduated from middle school to high school, that represented the fact that we passed middle school-level assignments and could now handle high school assignments.

In the same way, we encounter more advanced life situations. Sometimes, you may ask why this is happening in your life. Well, the answer may be simple: because you are ready.

However, this phase of things may require you to defy reason and logic and simply believe you can overcome. Therefore, do not be afraid or stop your progress. Let this phase shape your awareness that

> "The steadfast love of the LORD never ceases; his mercies never come to an end; they are new every morning;"

AND then digest Isaiah 41:10,

> "So do not fear, for I am with you; do not be dismayed, for I am your God. I will strengthen you and help you; I will uphold you with my righteous right hand."

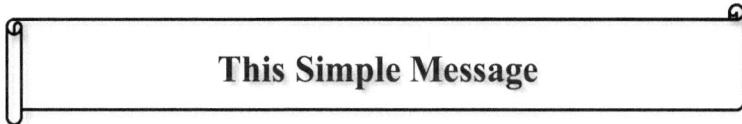
This Simple Message

"Peace, I leave with you; the peace I give to you. Not as the world gives do I give to you. Let not your hearts be troubled..."

~ John 14:27

How simple? This peace is known as peace beyond understanding. This principle is deep and probably deserves more written characters than this simple message. So, don't let our hearts be troubled. No matter our current struggle. In the presence of the Father is where that type of peace resides. We have an assurance of eternal peace from God.

Have a good week. 😊

Now, That's The Key

We've heard this before... Our Attitude Determines Our Altitude. Knowing who we are in God is the difference between getting by or soaring high. Therefore, we should challenge ourselves and do the opposite of our comfort zone. If our current situation needs a shake-up, then order a different flavor. You see, the people in the Bible who experienced the best miracles utilized their faith; they didn't wait to see who agreed. They simply moved by faith! However, it was radical faith.

Note, Ephesians 3:20 says,

> *"Now to him who is able to do immeasurably more than all we ask or imagine, according to his power that is at work within us.."*

Look at the last part: the power that works within us, including our faith. Now, that's the key.

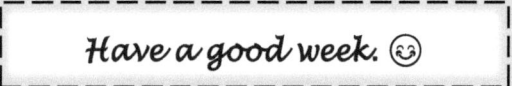

Grace Upon Grace, Favor Upon Favor

When Jesus fed five thousand people with a few loaves of bread and two fish, he first asked them to sit down. I found this to be quite insightful because it suggests that we should be at ease when seeking miracles. Settled. At peace.

Let us keep our passion alive. The adversary may try to discourage us, and we may experience intercession fatigue or even a sense of weariness from constant prayer and believing. During such moments, we can be content with the uncertainty, even going as far as not knowing what to pray for. Remember, the Holy Spirit intercedes when we don't know.

Rest in that.

Therefore, take a ride with the Master this week and ride easy. Grace upon grace and favor upon favor is among us.

Have a good week. ☺

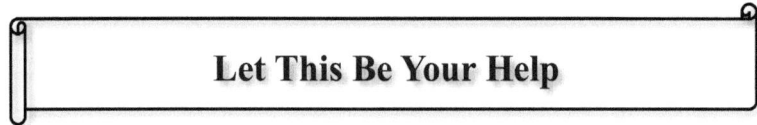

Let This Be Your Help

After performing all the positive steps outlined in self-help books, after quoting your positive affirmations, after crying and begging for change, and after you've done all you know to do, what should you do?

Wait for it... Just stand and stand firm. Even after thinking you can no longer cope. Stand. You may not be able to describe what you are going through, and even if you did, no one could understand. However, still stand. You see, God is looking at us and saying, I've given all you need to overcome this, yes, this situation. This situation is a part of my plan, and no need to overthink it.

Check out Ephesians 6: 13-14.

"Therefore put on the full armor of God, so that when the day of evil comes, you may be able to stand your ground, and after you have done everything, to stand... Stand firm"

Let that hit the spot and;

Have a good week. 😊

There Is A Scripture For That

Let us enter His gates with thanksgiving and His courts with praise; let us give thanks to Him and praise His name. (Psalm 100:4) It is essential for us to keep in mind that Christ came so we can live and live life more abundantly. (John 10:10) There is nothing that God will withhold from those who walk uprightly. (Psalm 84:11). As we can see, there is a scripture that supports our life narrative.

We are living by the Word, and we know the Word supports us. This week, let us understand that all things work together for good to those who love the Lord. (Romans 8:28). We will live in gratitude, praise, and knowing. For we know the plans God has for us, is to prosper us and not to harm us. To give us hope and a future. (Jeremiah 29:11.)

Drop Down and Give Me Fifty

"When you pass through the waters, I will be with you, and through the rivers, they shall not overwhelm you; when you walk through the fire, you shall not be burned, and the flame shall not consume you."

~ Isaiah 43:2.

This scripture reminds us that water, fire, and consumption will try us but shall not overtake us. There is no need to take ownership of these things when they show up. They are simply the proteins in our lives that build the muscle we need to carry our gifts. When the water and fire show up, just tell them to drop down and give me fifty. You are nothing but the muscle builder I need you to be.

Have a good week. 😊

Majority Rules

Challenged or Joyful or somewhere in-between? Stir Up Your Gift. In Matthew 6:9-13 we read,

Pray then like this: "Our Father in heaven, hallowed be your name. Your kingdom comes, you will be done, on earth as it is in heaven..."

On earth as it is in heaven, umm. What's in heaven? How does earth become like heaven? Well, a part of it is each one of us reaching for our inner gifting. It's by faith we know that we have a gift and purpose; and God has purposed us all. No matter where we are in life, it is not too early or too late!! Each gift has a purpose that glorifies the Father. Each gift is a piece of the puzzle that makes earth like heaven. So, stir up your gift. Don't let it burst out of season. It has value, and you know your value. Continuously praise your gift, even if it is as small as a mustard seed. No one else may recognize it but you and God. And that is a majority. Majority Rules!

Have a good week. ☺

Poetry Man

As I sing along to one of my favorite songs, *"Poetry Man"* by Phoebe Snow, the lyrics say, *'Talk to me some more. You don't have to go. You're the Poetry Man.'*

Those words perfectly describe the Holy Spirit's presence and His abilities; He makes life's challenges more meaningful, purposeful, and ultimately understandable. If living a life in fear, we may cancel out that understanding. But we can whisper quietly, you don't have to go, I want to talk to you some more. Your words are like poetry for my soul. Your direction is beautiful, and you make me laugh. Really, you don't have to go. Holy Spirit, you are my Poetry Man.

This week, just know that the Holy Spirit is always there to guide and support us. It's His eyes that light our night and provide our path. His eyes can see right through us. He is holding something very sweet, and let's take the time to ask Him to give it to us. He's like the Poetry Man. He makes things alright.

Our Greatest Tool

Who Is This Uncircumcised Philistine That Should Defy The People Of God?

In the scriptures, this was a bold question asked by King David to the people of God, who were being tormented and perplexed by this larger-than-life predator named Goliath. As the story goes, David, in faith with his small hand tool, defeated the largest agitator of that time.

Don't allow sickness, fear, lack, or anything to be an unconquerable bully in our lives. Speak to the "Philistine (s)" in our life with the same confidence as David. Take our position with our Greatest Tool, which is our raised hands in praise and thanksgiving. Just as instructed in Colossians 4:2, "Devote yourselves to prayer, being watchful and thankful." Then, see the manifestation of the Lord as He conquers that which appeared unchangeable, scary and stifling. Our hands raised in praise, is our greatest tool.

Have a good week. 😊

www.ingramcontent.com/pod-product-compliance
Lightning Source LLC
Chambersburg PA
CBHW041808040426
42449CB00001B/13